SCIENCE-*OLOGY*

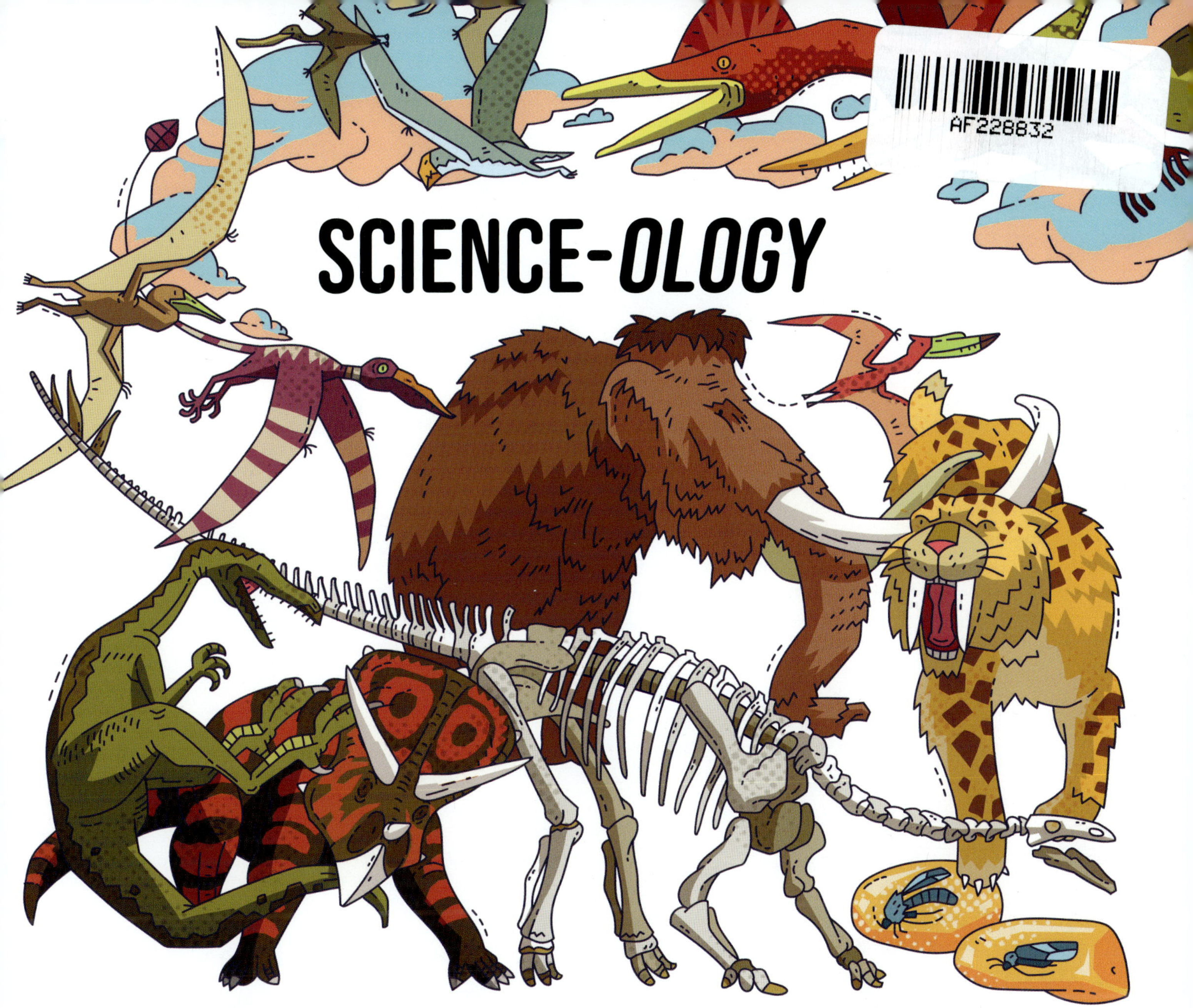

PALEONTOLOGY

ANNA CLAYBOURNE
DANIEL LIMÓN

PowerKiDS press

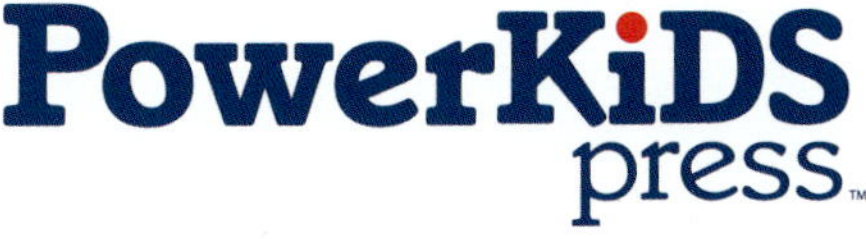

Published in 2026 by The Rosen Publishing Group, Inc.
2544 Clinton Street, Buffalo, NY 14224

First published in Great Britain in 2023 by Wayland
Copyright © Hodder and Stoughton, 2023

Editor: Elise Short
Consultant: Dr Stig A. Walsh, Senior Curator of Vertebrate Palaeobiology at National Museums Scotland
Design: Rocket Design (East Anglia) Ltd
Illustrations: Daniel Limón

Cataloging-in-Publication Data
Names: Claybourne, Anna, author. | Limón, Daniel Sanchez, illustrator.
Title: Paleontology / by Anna Claybourne, illustrated by Daniel Limón.
Description: Buffalo, NY : PowerKids Press, 2026. | Series: Science-ology |
  Includes glossary and index.
Identifiers: ISBN 9781499454789 (pbk.) | ISBN 9781499454796 (library bound) |
  ISBN 9781499454802 (ebook)
Subjects: LCSH: Paleontology--Juvenile literature.
Classification: LCC QE714.5 C539 2026 | DDC 560--dc23

Picture credits: Alamy: Ellena Aponte/Reuters 45tr; Lou Linwei 45cr; Pictorial Press 9b.
Science Photo Library 38t; Suddeutsche Zeitung Photo 41b.
Vintage Book Collection 17t.
Dreamstime: Antonella865 19b.
Science Photo Library: Pascal Goetgheluck 38b; NHM/London 24t, 27br.
Shutterstock: Ad hominem 20t; Atlaspix 37tr; Thomas Barrat 4t; Alex Coan 7br; Catmando 17b; Dinoton 7bc; Dotted yeti 21cl; Daniel Eskridge 32b; FotoHelin 15bl; Gluiki 5bcl, 11b; Aldona Griskeviciene 35br;Herschel Hoffmeyer 17c; Carolina Jaramillo 14b; Peter Jozefek 8bl; Breck P Kent 15t; Mark Kostich 29b; Luca Lonzarelli 42b; Macrovector 7t; Gil Cohen Magen 28b; Lev Radin 29t;SciePro 21c, 21cr, 21bl; Sensvector 6t; Roni Setiawan 5br; Eugen Thome 5bl; Vac1 15br; vectorlife 19t; Kriengsak Wiriyakrieng 27r; Wlad74 11tr; YuRi Photolife 13t. Shutterstock editorial: Amblin/Legendary/Universal/Kobal: 41t.
Wellcome Collection, London: 11tl.
Wikimedia Commons: Everard Home 11c; Hans A Rosbach 9t; James St John 21t;
Yuyu Tamai 30b; Gary Todd 37cr.

Manufactured in the United States of America
CPSIA Compliance Information: Batch #CSPK26. For further information contact Rosen Publishing at 1-800-237-9932.

CONTENTS

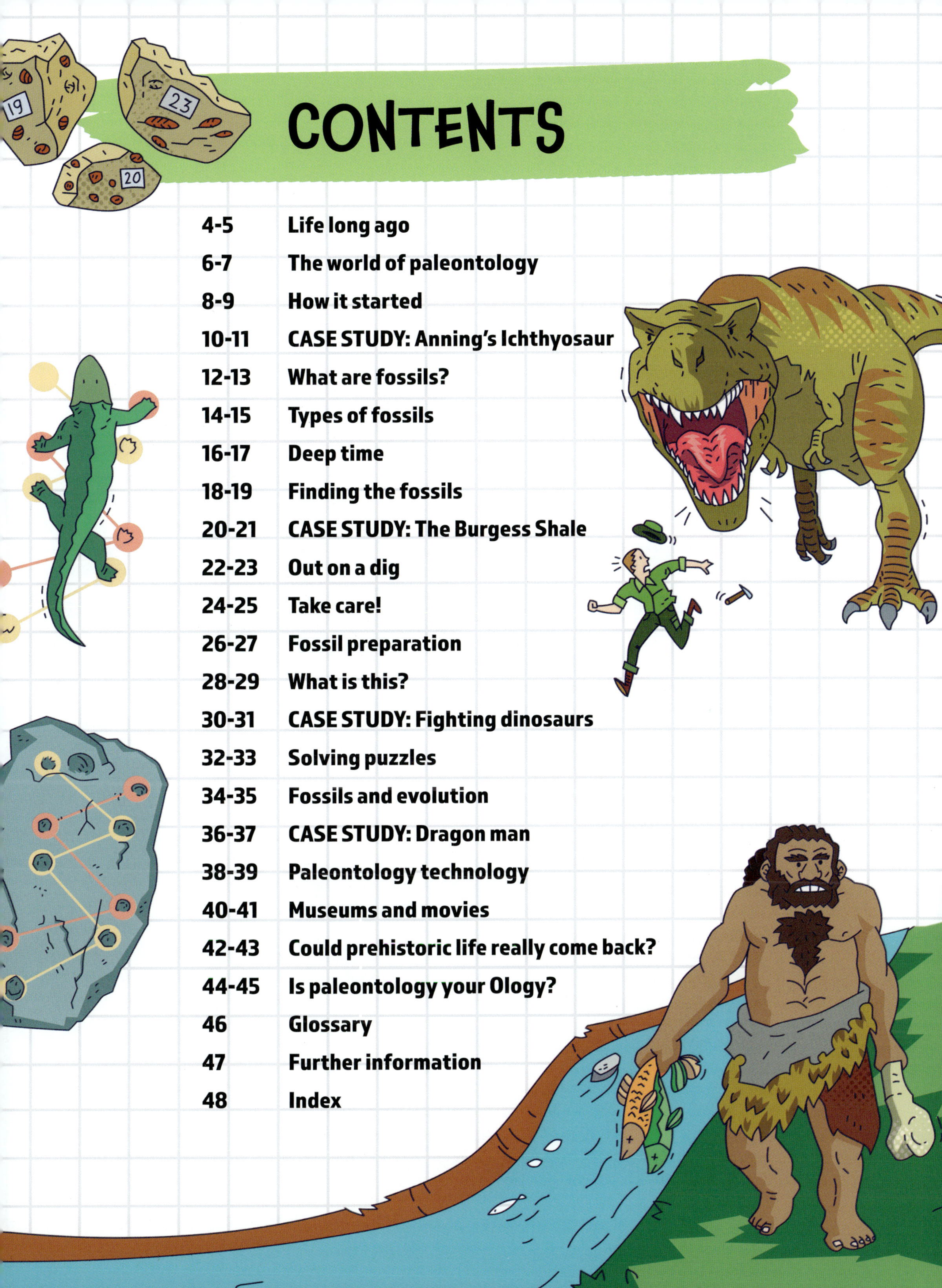

LIFE LONG AGO

Do you love fossils, dinosaurs, and other prehistoric creatures? Then you'll love paleontology! It's the study of living things from long ago, and the fossils, footprints, and other traces they left behind.

Dinosaur fossils ...

When people think of paleontology and fossils, they often think of dinosaurs. That's not surprising, because dinosaurs are incredible, and everyone's heard of them.

... and other fossils too!

However, paleontology is about more than dinosaurs – a lot more! The dinosaurs lived from around 240 million years ago to 66 million years ago. But there are fossils that date back billions of years, revealing all kinds of ancient creatures that lived long before the dinosaurs existed. And many other species, or types, of living things lived alongside them, and after them too.

This fossil *Tyrannosaurus rex* is named Sue after Sue Hendrickson, the fossil hunter who found it. It is over 40 feet (12 m) long from nose to tail.

How long ago?

Paleontologists study the fossils of all kinds of different living things from many different time periods. Here are just a few of them ...

- Ancient microfossils, or microscopic fossils, of early bacteria-like life

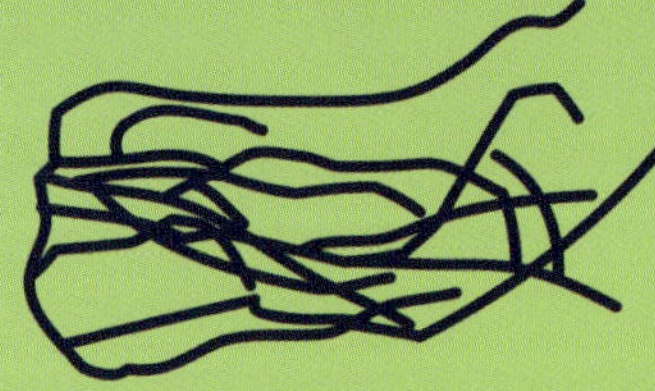

- Tiny fossils of the oldest known seaweed

Like many other types of science, paleontology has a name ending in "ology." It comes from several old Greek words, and means "the study of old beings."

PALAIOS = old

+

ONTO = being

+

LOGY = study

DID YOU KNOW?

Over time, old species die out and become extinct, and new ones develop, or evolve.

Scientists think that at 99 percent of all the species that have ever existed are now extinct!

500 million years ago

- Trilobites, creepy-crawly sea creatures related to insects and crabs

161 million years ago

- Dinosaurs, such as *Ceratosaurus*, *Diplodocus*, and *Stegosaurus*

4 million years ago

- *Dromornis stirtoni*, or Stirton's Thunderbird, a tall flightless bird

100,000 years ago

- Neanderthals, early humans who were a different species from us.

THE WORLD OF PALEONTOLOGY

What's it like being a paleontologist? It depends! There are many different types of paleontology, and most paleontologists have to do a range of different things as part of their job.

Digging up fossils

Most paleontologists spend some time outdoors on digs, looking for and digging up interesting fossils. They may have to travel a long way to the best fossil hunting spots.

Lab work

In the lab, paleontologists study and work with the fossils they've found.

That could include ...

- Figuring out how broken fossil parts or skeletons fit together

- Comparing a new discovery to other fossils or the bones of living animals, to help decide what it is

- Using microscopes and scanners to get a close look at a fossil, or even inside it

- Using evidence from fossils to figure out what a species was like when it was alive, or how it evolved over time.

Teaching

A lot of paleontologists work in universities, where they teach students how to do paleontology, lab work, and fossil digs.

Writing and presenting

Paleontologists have to keep notes and records about what they find, and write about their discoveries. They also give talks at science conferences and meetings.

- ## • Museum work

Some paleontologists work in museums, looking after fossil collections and preparing interesting displays.

- ## • You're on TV!

And some help to make TV shows or films about fossils or prehistoric animals, or write books about them.

Areas and branches

Paleontology is a huge area of science, covering billions of years of time, and countless different species. So most paleontologists don't study all of it. Instead, they usually focus on a particular type or area of paleontology.

For example, you might be interested in ...

 **Paleobotany** – plant fossils

 **Paleozoology** – animal fossils

 **Vertebrate paleontology** – vertebrates, or animals with backbones, such as fish and horses

 **Invertebrate paleontology** – invertebrates, such as insects, spiders and worms

 **Micropaleontology** – microscopic fossils, such as fossilized single-celled animals

 **Human paleontology** – human fossils

Or a special area, such as ...

- **Paleoecology** – what fossils reveal about how species lived together in their habitats

- **Paleoclimatology** – what fossils reveal about prehistoric weather and climate

- **Taphonomy** – how fossils form and become altered over time

- **Ichnology** – the study of trace fossils (see page 14), such as footprints, tracks, burrows, and fossilized poop!

A dinosaur coprolite, or fossil poop

A two-million-year-old fossil skull of Australopithecus, an ancient relative of humans

HOW IT STARTED

Humans have been finding fossils in the ground for thousands of years. But it took us a long time to understand what they really meant.

Monsters and magic

Long ago, when people found fossils that looked like unknown animals, they sometimes thought they must be proof of magical creatures, such as dragons or giants. In fact, this could help to explain some traditional myths and legends.

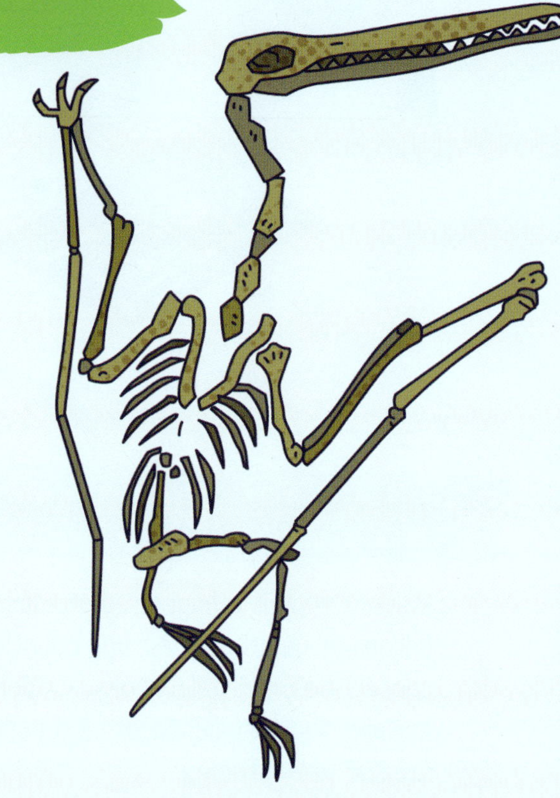

There are traditional tales of dragons all over the world, which could be based on dinosaur and pterosaur fossils.

Some people thought that fossils were animals or plants that had been turned to stone, perhaps by witches or fairies. Belemnites, which are fossils of extinct squid-like animals, were called "thunderbolts," said to be created when lightning struck the ground.

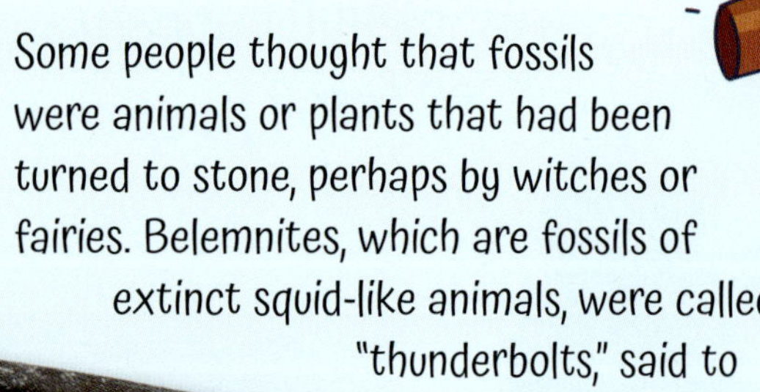

Understanding fossils

However, some people did realize that fossils must be the remains of real living things. Over 2,500 years ago, ancient Greek philosopher Xenophanes realized that seashell and fish fossils on land meant that the land must have once been covered by water.

In the 1000s, Chinese scientist Shen Kuo had similar ideas. He saw that fossilized seashells on land showed that land and rocks could move around over time.

Meanwhile, Persian scientist Ibn Sina thought there must be a natural process that turned real creatures into stony fossils, which he called "petrifying fluid."

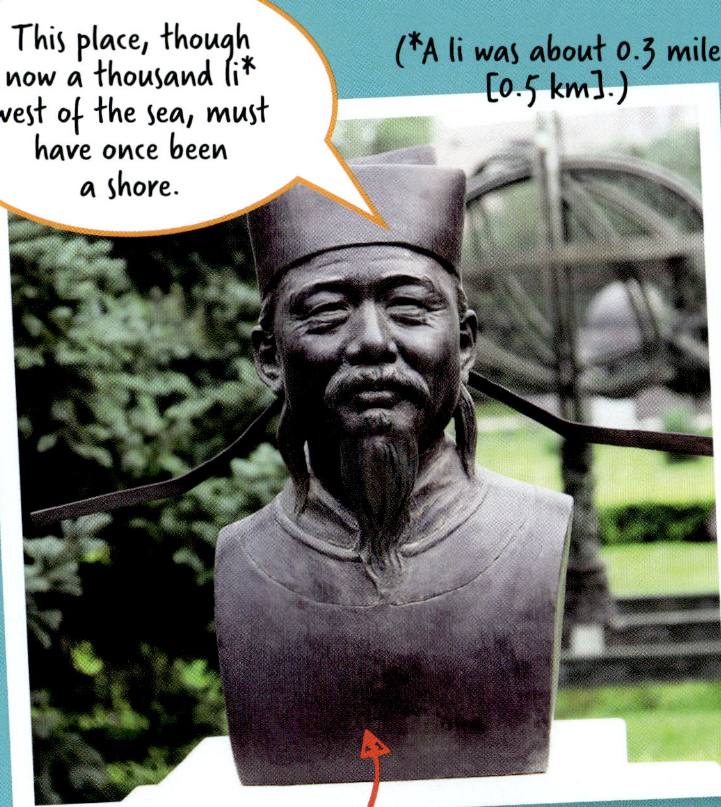

(*A li was about 0.3 mile [0.5 km].)

Shen Kuo

A new science

From the 1500s onwards, more and more scientists, such as Leonardo da Vinci and Nicolas Steno, collected and studied fossils. In the early 1800s, leading French naturalist Georges Cuvier argued that fossils proved that many once-living species had become extinct.

Through the 1800s, paleontology became a popular craze, thanks to fossil hunters and scientists such as Cuvier, Mary Anning, and William Buckland. By the 1900s, it was recognized everywhere as an important science.

Georges Cuvier made detailed drawings of fossils and gave lectures about them.

Anning's Ichthyosaur

In the year 1812, at just 12 years old, Mary Anning finished digging a fabulous, 16-foot- (5 m) long fossil monster out of the cliffs near her home. She is now one of the most famous fossil hunters in history.

Mary found thousands of fossils on the beaches and cliffs around Lyme Regis, England, her hometown.

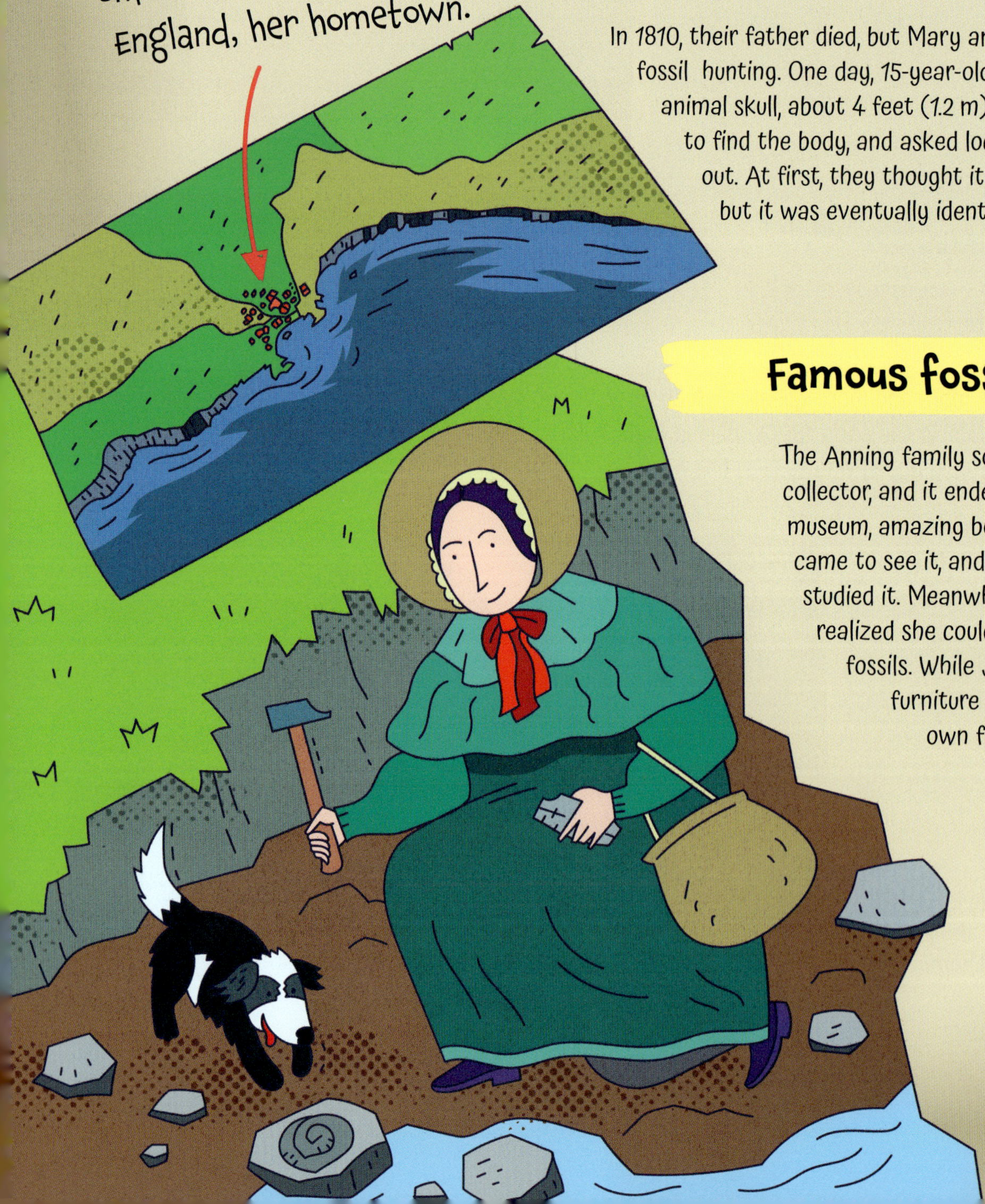

Mary Anning was born into a poor family in Lyme Regis, on the south coast of England, in 1799. When she was small, Mary and her older brother Joseph often helped their father search for fossils to sell to make some extra money.

In 1810, their father died, but Mary and Joseph still went fossil hunting. One day, 15-year-old Joseph found a large animal skull, about 4 feet (1.2 m) long. Mary went back to find the body, and asked locals to help her dig it out. At first, they thought it looked like a crocodile, but it was eventually identified as an ichthyosaur.

Famous fossil finder

The Anning family sold the fossil to a collector, and it ended up in a London museum, amazing both the public who came to see it, and paleontologists who studied it. Meanwhile, Mary Anning realized she could make a living selling fossils. While Joseph became a furniture maker, she set up her own fossil shop.

Mary Anning went fossil hunting almost every day with her dog, Tray.

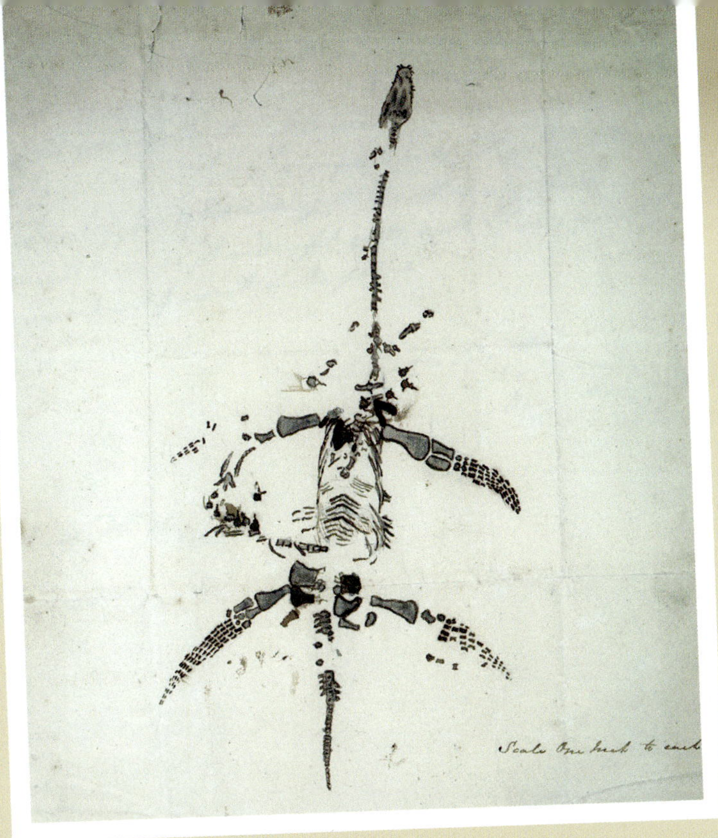

Anning often found small ammonites, belemnites, and fish fossils to sell. But every so often, she unearthed much bigger and rarer fossils. She became famous for the ichthyosaurs, plesiosaurs, and pterosaurs (see page 33) she discovered. Leading fossil scientists of the time often came to visit her and bought fossils from her to study.

Anning also made her own notes and drawings of her fossils, like this plesiosaur from 1824, and became an expert on prehistoric sea creatures.

Today, the rest of the ichthyosaur Anning dug up when she was 12 has been lost, and only the skull survives.

WHAT ARE ICHTHYOSAURS?

The name ichthyosaur means "fish-lizard." They were not fish, but fish-shaped hunting sea reptiles. The biggest ichthyosaurs could reach 70 feet (21 m) long. They lived around the same time as the early dinosaurs.

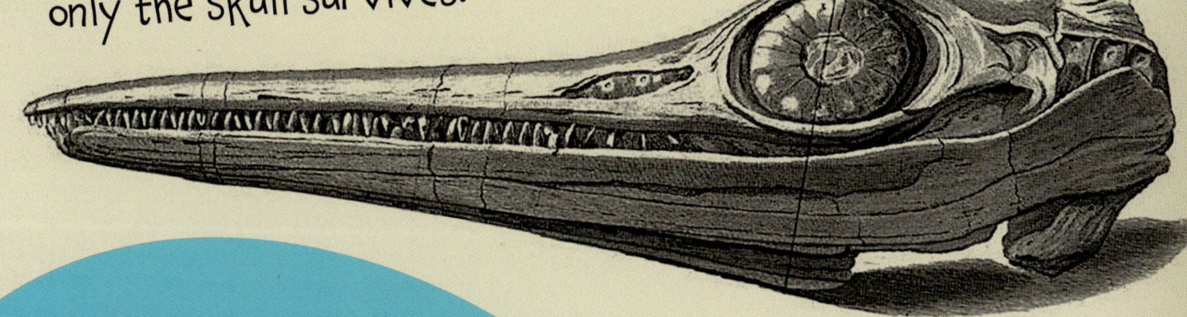

FACT FILE

ANNING'S ICHTHYOSAUR

NAME: *TEMNODONTOSAURUS PLATYODON*

LIVED: AROUND 195 MILLION YEARS AGO

LENGTH: 17 FEET (5.2 M)

DISCOVERED: 1811-1812

WHAT ARE FOSSILS?

You probably know that most fossils are made of stone, in the shapes of skeletons, shells, leaves, or other things that were once alive. But how exactly did those things turn to stone?

Formation of a fossil

These pictures show one of the most common ways a fossil can form, known as "permineralization."

Millions of years in the past, a fish dies and sinks onto the seabed.

1

2

Its soft body rots away or gets eaten by other sea creatures, leaving just a skeleton.

Layers of mud or sand collect on top.

3

How do we know?

For centuries, no one was sure how living things could be petrified, or turned to stone. One of the first people to figure it out was English scientist Robert Hooke in the 1660s.

Looking at fossilized wood through a microscope, Hooke saw that it had the same tiny patterns as normal wood, but made from minerals. He realized that this could have happened as water soaked into the wood, carrying dissolved minerals with it – and the same thing could happen to bones and shells too.

What gets fossilized?

Not all living things become fossils – in fact, very few do. Most fossils form in layers of sediment at the bottom of seas and lakes. So it's usually water creatures that get fossilized, or sometimes plants or animals that fell into the water when they died.

It's also rare for soft body parts to be fossilized, as they usually rot away too fast. So there are lots of fossils of hard things such as bones, shells, insects, crabs, and pine cones, but not so many worms, mushrooms, or jellyfish.

Crabs are often preserved as fossils, as they are sea creatures and have hard shells.

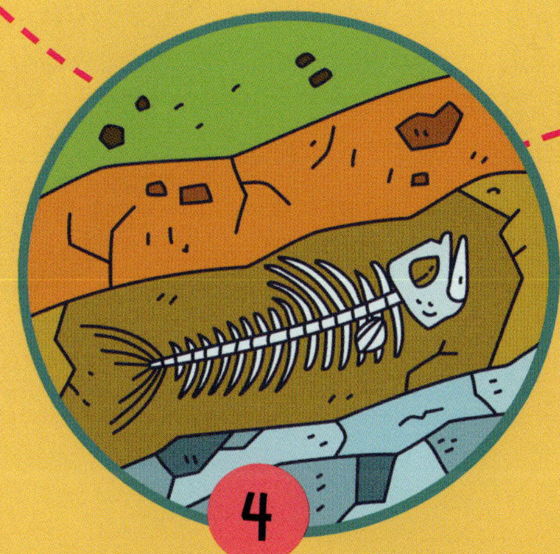

4 Over time, the layers get squashed down and harden into layers of solid rock, called sedimentary rock.

5 Water containing dissolved minerals soaks through the rock and the skeleton trapped inside. It deposits minerals, which build up in spaces in the bones.

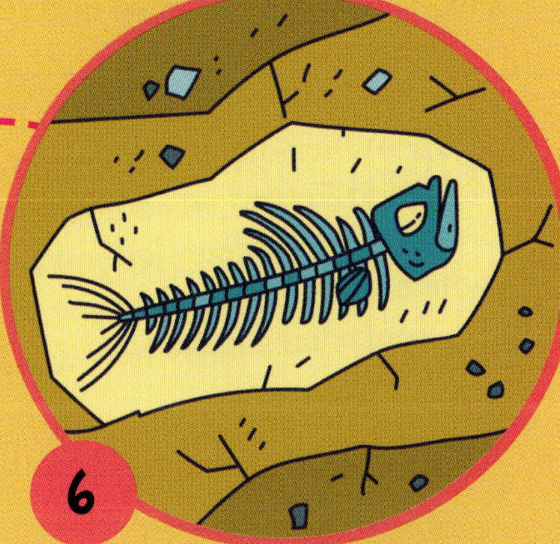

6 Sometimes, the water dissolves all the bone, and replaces it with minerals. The skeleton is now a stone fossil.

HOW LONG DOES IT TAKE?

It's possible for fossils to form in just a few months or years, in the right situation – but it usually happens over thousands or millions of years.

TYPES OF FOSSILS

Trace fossils

Trace fossils are fossilized marks or imprints. That means things like footprints, skin imprints, burrows, or trails left by a worm or snake slithering along, or even a dinosaur's tail dragging along the ground. The marks were made in sand, mud, or clay that later hardened into rock.

395-million-year-old fossil footprints found in Poland were made by an early tetrapod, or four-legged amphibian, which evolved from a type of fish. The footprints show how it walked.

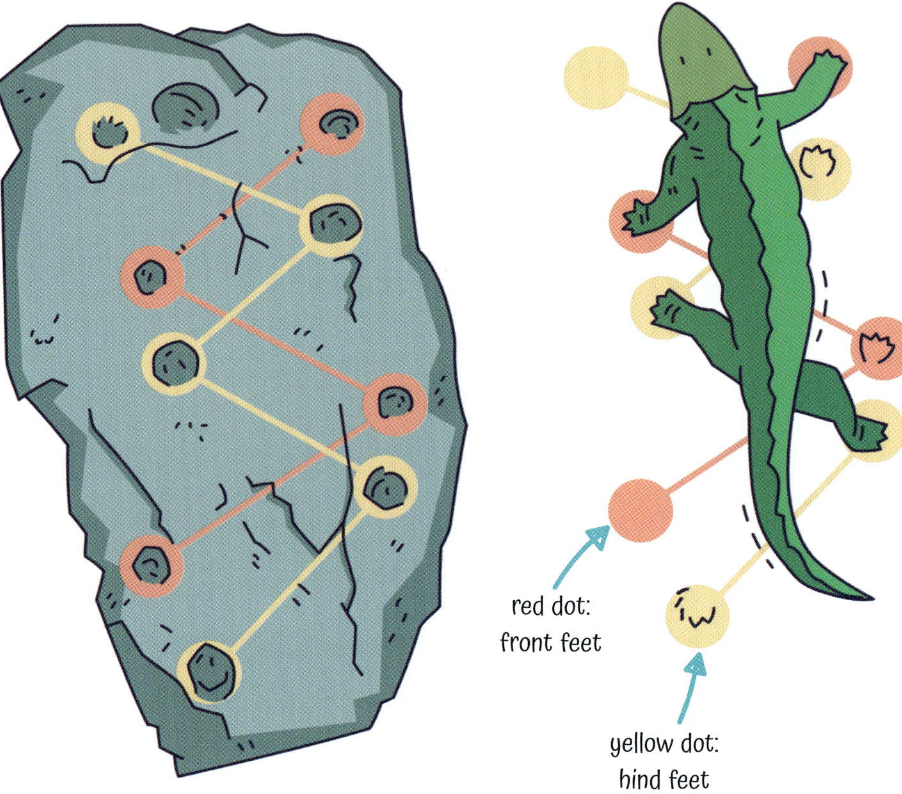

Molds and casts

Sometimes, a shell or skeleton gets trapped in layers of rock, then dissolves away and leaves an empty space, called a mold fossil. If the empty mold gets filled in with minerals or sediments later, it makes a solid copy of the animal's shape, called a cast. The molds themselves are called impressions.

An ammonite mold fossil

If a plant or animal gets trapped between layers of rock, it sometimes gets squished flat. As layers build up on top, it can get squished so hard that it heats up. This "cooks" the chemicals until only the black carbon, which is found in all living things, is left behind. A dark carbon film or "print" of the living thing is left on the stone. This is also how the fossil fuel coal is formed.

Leaves are often fossilized as carbon films.

Unaltered remains

Unaltered remains are dead creatures that have been preserved for a long time without turning to stone or rotting away. This could happen if the creature fell into a peat bog, which contains acid that preserves soft body parts but dissolves the bones (a bit like a jar of pickled fish). Or it could be frozen in ice, like food in a deep freezer, which stops it from rotting away.

Sometimes, small animals like insects or spiders get trapped in a thick, sticky resin released by conifer trees. The resin then fossilizes, becoming hard, golden amber, with the animal still inside.

A fly, millions of years old, trapped in amber

DEEP-FROZEN MAMMOTH

In 2007, a reindeer herder in the far north of Russia found a frozen animal near a river bank. It turned out to be an amazingly well-preserved 42,000-year-old mammoth calf, complete with skin, fur, eyes, and trunk. Paleontologists found that the mammoth, nicknamed Lyuba, had drowned in mud, which probably preserved it for a while before it froze.

DEEP TIME

Deep time, also called geological time, is the unimaginably huge duration of time since the Earth formed. It's revealed in the layers of rocks that have formed over billions of years, and the fossils found in them.

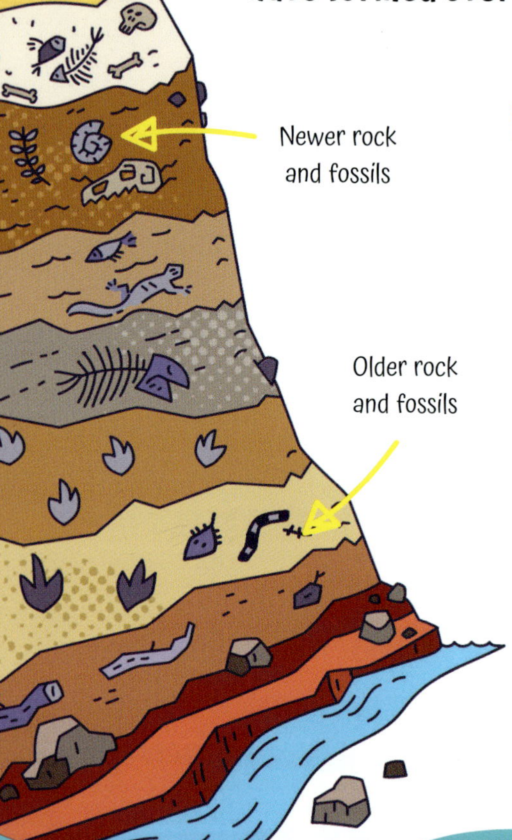

How it works

Fossils mainly form in sedimentary rocks, which are laid down over time in layers called strata. Deeper strata are made of older rock, and contain older fossils.

Over millions of years, rocks wear away, break apart, tilt, and move around. So there is no "complete" set of rock layers, containing the whole of Earth's history in one place. But there are similar patterns of fossils and rock strata in different places. By matching them up, paleontologists create a chart or calendar of the ages of different rocks and fossils, called the fossil record.

Index fossils

Index fossils are widespread, easy-to-spot fossils that are used to date rocks and other fossils. For example, *Mucrospirifer mucronatus* fossil seashells were around from 416 to 359 million years ago. So if you find them, you know that's how old the rocks are.

Dating rocks and fossils

Rocks and fossils often contain traces of radioactive minerals, such as potassium or uranium. Some of their atoms slowly change or decay over time. By measuring what proportion of atoms have changed, you can find out how much time has passed since they formed. Scientists use this method, called radiometric dating, to find the ages of some types of rock strata.

"STRATA" SMITH

One of the first people to discover how rock strata work was British geologist William Smith. In the late 1700s, he was working as a surveyor, finding good places to put canals or mines. He was also a fossil collector, and noticed how rocks and fossils formed the same patterns of layers, even in different places.

Smith made the first charts and maps showing rock strata, such as his famous 1815 rock map of England. His work earned him the nickname "Strata Smith."

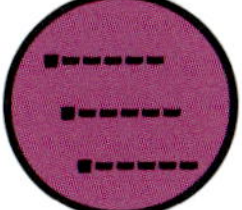

Deep time chart

Put all these things together, and you can create a chart of deep time, like this. It's divided into sections, called eons, eras, periods, and epochs.

EON	ERA	PERIOD	EPOCH
Phanerozoic	Cenozoic	Quaternary	Holocene
			Pleistocene
			Pliocene
		Neogene	Miocene
			Oligocene
		Paleogene	Eocene
			Paleocene
	Mesozoic	Cretaceous	
		Jurassic	
		Triassic	
	Paleozoic	Permian	
		Carboniferous	
		Devonian	
		Silurian	
		Ordovician	
		Cambrian	
Proterozoic			
Archaean			
Hadean			

Younger → / Older ←

Tyrannosaurus rex lived in the late Cretaceous Period.

The first fish evolved in the Cambrian Period.

The Hadean Eon was the time before life began.

FINDING THE FOSSILS

The right rocks

Fossils have been found all over the world, but if you want to find a particular type of fossil, you have to find the right type of rock. For example, suppose you were looking for early bird fossils, to find out more about how birds evolved from dinosaurs. You would be most likely to find these in sedimentary rocks from the late Jurassic and early Cretaceous periods, around 150 million years ago.

You'd look at geological rock maps and ground scans to find these rocks. You could also choose places where other early bird fossils have been found, as that might give you a better chance.

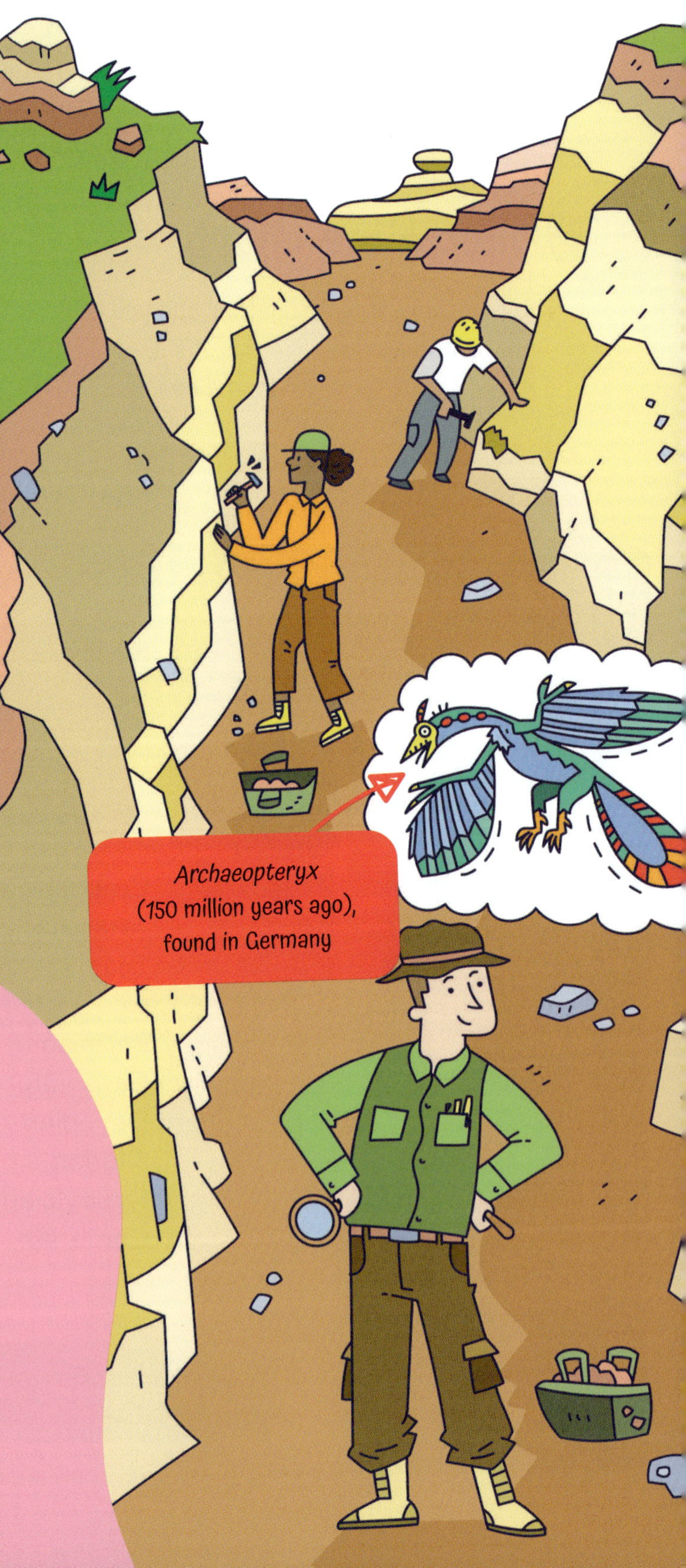

The best spots

You're most likely to find fossils at places where rocks are exposed, revealing the rock strata. Seaside cliffs, mountains, old quarries, and canyons, where rivers have cut deep channels through rock, are all good places to start a fossil hunt.

Over centuries of fossil hunting, paleontologists have found fossil hotspots around the world, and they're still exploring many of them. You can see a few of them on this map.

Look what I've found!

Sometimes, it's not a paleontologist but a farmer, miner, or passing hiker who finds a fossil, leading to an amazing discovery. This happened in Argentina in 2012, when shepherd Aurelio Hernandez found a huge fossil bone on the ranch where he was working. His boss called paleontologists to investigate, and they found a new species of dinosaur, *Patagotitan mayorum*, one of the biggest ever discovered.

Patagotitan mayorum

GET PERMISSION!

Even when you're sure you've found the perfect site, you can't just start digging. First, you have to get permission from the landowner or government that owns the land. There may be laws that mean any fossil you find belongs to them, and has to be returned to them after you've studied it.

The Burgess Shale

Besides looking for new fossils, paleontologists also study old fossil collections in museums and universities. Sometimes, they find something amazing! That's what happened in the famous case of the Burgess Shale.

Fabulous fossil find

In 1909, paleontologist Charles Walcott was exploring in Canada's Rocky Mountains when he found a new fossil site near Mount Burgess. Layers of shale rock were filled with fascinating fossils of sea worms, trilobites, shrimp-like animals, and many more.

Walcott knew the fossils were special, as they included soft body parts, which are rarely fossilized. They were also very old, dating from around 508 million years ago, long before the dinosaurs, or even the first land animals.

Experts think an undersea mudslide killed and trapped the animals of the Burgess Shale and somehow stopped them from decaying, allowing their soft parts to be fossilized.

Another look

For the next 15 years, Walcott collected over 65,000 Burgess Shale fossils, and sorted them into groups of animals that were already known about, such as jellyfish and sea cucumbers. After he died in 1927, they stayed stored away for over 30 years.

Then, in the 1960s, paleontologists began to look at the fossils again. To their astonishment, they found strange, unfamiliar creatures. There were whole new groups of living things, previously unknown to science, including some very odd-looking creatures.

Eldonia fossil from the Burgess Shale

Meet the creatures

- Here are just a few of the most famous creatures of the Burgess Shale:

  - *Opabinia*

  - *Ottoia*

  - *Marella*

- *Hallucigenia* – at first no one knew which were its spines and which were its legs!

OUT ON A DIG

Paleontologists don't spend all their time digging up fossils, but they do get to do it sometimes. It's called being on a dig or excavation, or working "in the field."

Excavating fossils

There are several different methods of excavating fossils, depending on their size and the type of rock they're in.

• Large fossils

Something like a giant dinosaur leg bone is too big for someone to lift. You have to use shovels, a jackhammer, or even a small digger to dig around and under it. If it's really big, you might even need a crane or helicopter to lift it out of the ground.

• Small fossils

You can sometimes pick small fossils such as shark teeth or a tiny ammonite out of loose rock or sand. Sometimes paleontologists sieve sand or crumbly rock to find small fossils, or wash lumps of rock in water to separate out the fossils.

PALEONTOLOGIST'S TOOLKIT

Each paleontologist has their own set of tools and supplies for working in the field. Here are some of the main essentials:

Rock hammer

Chisels

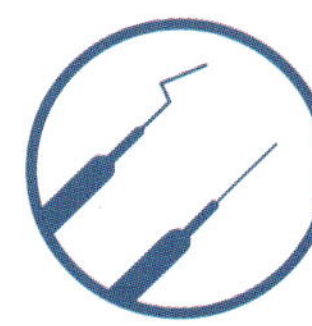
Dental picks

Brushes

Tape measure

mini magnifying glass

Notebook and pencils

Sample bags and labels

GPS and Walkie-talkies

Multi-tool

• Medium fossils

If a larger fossil is stuck in the rock, you can often chip away the stone around it with a hammer, pick, or chisel, or gently clean it with a brush or pointed tool. With smaller fossils, you can sometimes dig out the piece of rock around the fossil, and take it back to the lab to work on.

Staying on site

Fossil sites are often a long way from where you normally work, and it can take a long time to dig out the fossils. So paleontologists usually go on a field trip in a group, and stay for several days or weeks. They might live in a hotel if there is one, but in remote places, they usually stay with locals or camp in tents.

TAKE CARE!

When you're digging for and excavating fossils, you always have to be very, very careful. Rocks and fossils can be fragile, and so can you!

Protect that fossil!

Most fossils are made of rock, but they're not always "rock-hard." They can be very delicate, breakable, or sometimes already broken. When you're excavating and moving them, you have to try to keep them intact and make sure they don't break any more. Paleontologists have a few techniques to help with this:

• Glue it

Special dissolvable glue is used to coat delicate fossils or hold broken fossil bits together.

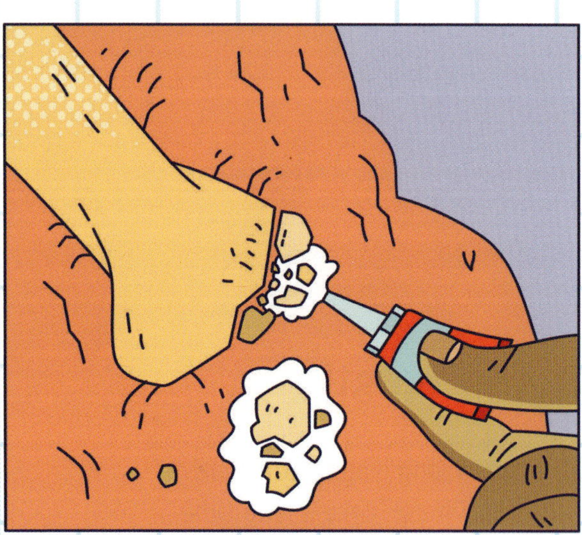

• Give it a jacket!

Bigger fossils are sometimes wrapped in cloth and coated with plaster, which then sets hard. It's just like a plaster cast for a broken leg, but in paleontology it's known as a "jacket."

• Wrap it up

You can use tissue paper, newspaper, paper bags, foil, foam sheets, or bubble-wrap to wrap fossils up safely, held in place by elastic bands or tape.

Notes and labels

You also have to label each fossil you collect with its own number, and make detailed notes about it. This could be vital for understanding more about the living thing, such as when it died and how it was fossilized.

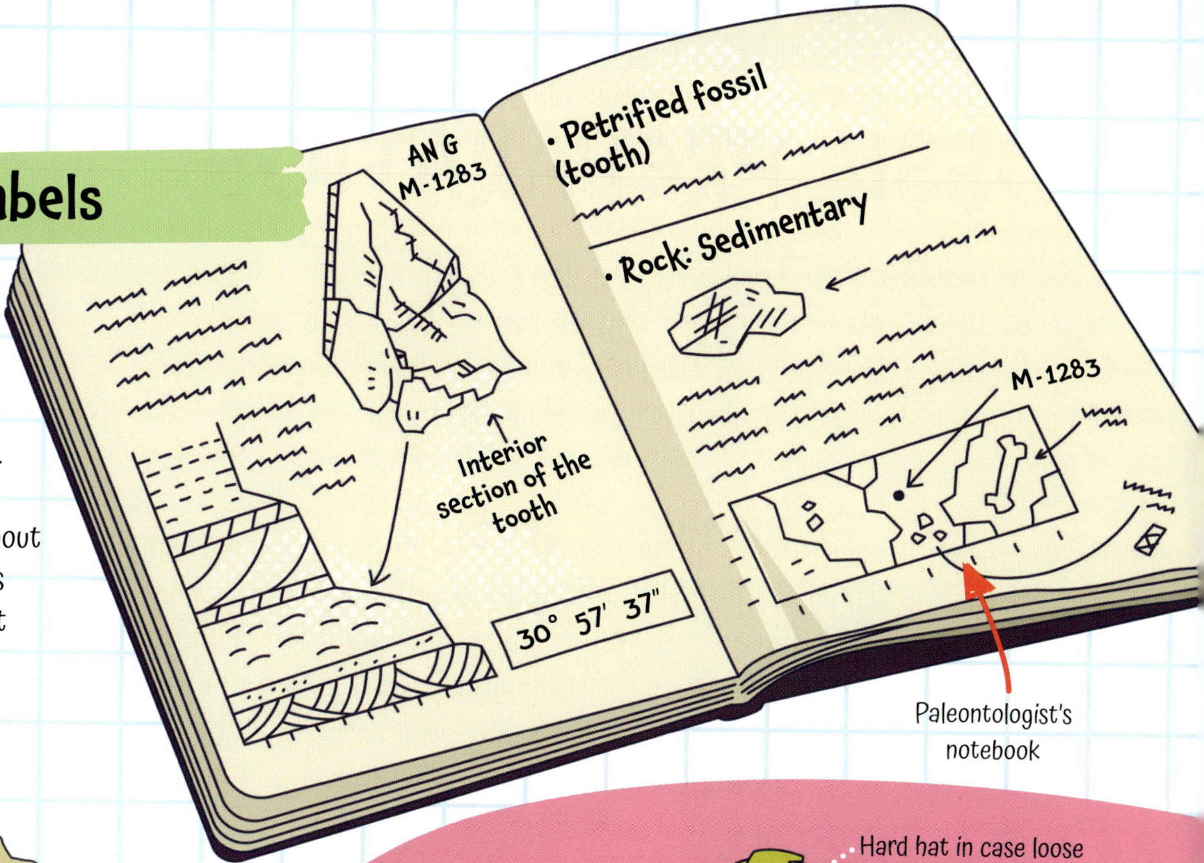

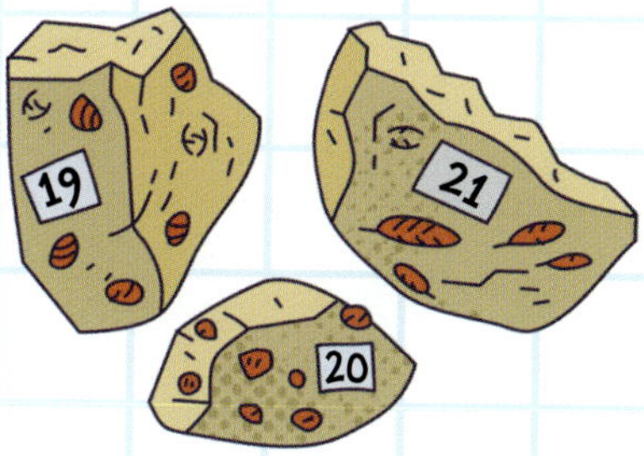

SAFETY FIRST!

Fossils are often found in cliffs and mountain areas, riverbanks, in caves, and on beaches, all places that can be dangerous. So paleontologists have to be sensible and careful – for example, don't be tempted to scramble up a cliff without safety gear to reach a good fossil! You also need to know how to use power tools such as drills and jackhammers safely, and how to move heavy rocks without hurting yourself.

You might need safety gear like this too, depending on where you're working.

FOSSIL PREPARATION

After being collected, fossils go back to the lab to be "prepared." That means cleaning them up, repairing them, and getting them ready to be studied.

Preparation station

Fossil preparation is done by a preparator in a special preparation lab that has tools for doing all the different preparation jobs. These tasks include ...

• Unpacking

Removing the protective glue, wrapping, or plaster jacket from a fossil without damaging it. This preparator is using a power saw to cut through the jacket.

This machine is sucking up the dust from cutting through the plaster jacket.

• Delicate cleaning

The next step is cleaning away the last scraps of rock and dust from the fossil surface. Preparators use special tools for this, such as an air scribe, which uses compressed air to make a needlelike tip vibrate.

• Making repairs

If a fossil is chipped or broken, preparators use glues or resins to fix the parts together. Sometimes they use filler to replace lost fossil material.

BEING A PREPARATOR

The paleontologist who found a fossil can sometimes do the preparation work themselves, but it takes a long time and special skills. So labs also have teams of full-time preparators, whose main job is cleaning up and preparing fossils.

A preparator at work on a dinosaur fossil in Maha Sarakham, Thailand

• Removing the matrix

The matrix is the rock surrounding or covering the fossil. Preparators use small drills, chisels, or awls to break away larger pieces of rock.

• Making casts

Once the fossil is cleaned up and ready, preparators often make casts of it. They coat it in rubbery material that dries solid, then peels off. This can then be used as a mold to make exact copies of the fossil. The copies can be sent to museums to display, or to paleontologists around the world, so they can all look at the fossil.

Ready to study!

Now the fossil, or a copy of it, is ready for studying. Paleontologists might start work on it right away, especially if it seems like an important fossil or a new species. Or they might store the fossil as part of a collection. They give each fossil its own ID number and label, and record it in a list or catalogue, so that everyone knows where to find the fossils they need.

A horse tooth fossil labeled with an ID code

WHAT IS THIS?

When you find a fossil, one of the first things you have to do is figure out what type and species of living thing it is – or was!

Looks familiar?

Paleontologists often find fossils of species they already know about – such as a small *Androgynoceras* ammonite, for example.

It's not a major discovery, but it could still be interesting. Maybe it's in an area it hasn't been found in before, revealing new information about the species. Or it could be an unusually large or small example. Even if there's nothing unusual about it, it could be useful for students to study, or it might make a nice museum display.

Fossils of early humans are often found in separate parts. You might find a skull and upper jaw in one place, and a lower jaw somewhere else. If they are the same age and clearly fit together, you have a whole skull!

 ## Jigsaw pieces

Sometimes, you might find a fossil that fits together with another that's already been found. They might not be from the same individual living thing, but they can help to build up a picture of what that species was like.

A new species!

If you compare your new find to all other similar fossils, and it's different, it could be a totally new species. When this happens, you write a paper, or science report, describing the new fossil, and giving it a name. Like species living today, each fossil species has its own two-part scientific name, written in Latin.

Sir David Attenborough

A new beetle

In 2021, paleontologists figured out that this 49-million-year-old beetle fossil was a new species and gave it the name:

Pulchritudo attenboroughi

A scientific name has two parts, and usually describes the animal in some way.

This part means "beauty."

★ **Scientific names are always written in *italics*!**

★ **The first part has a capital letter.**

This part is named after the famous naturalist and wildlife broadcaster Sir David Attenborough.

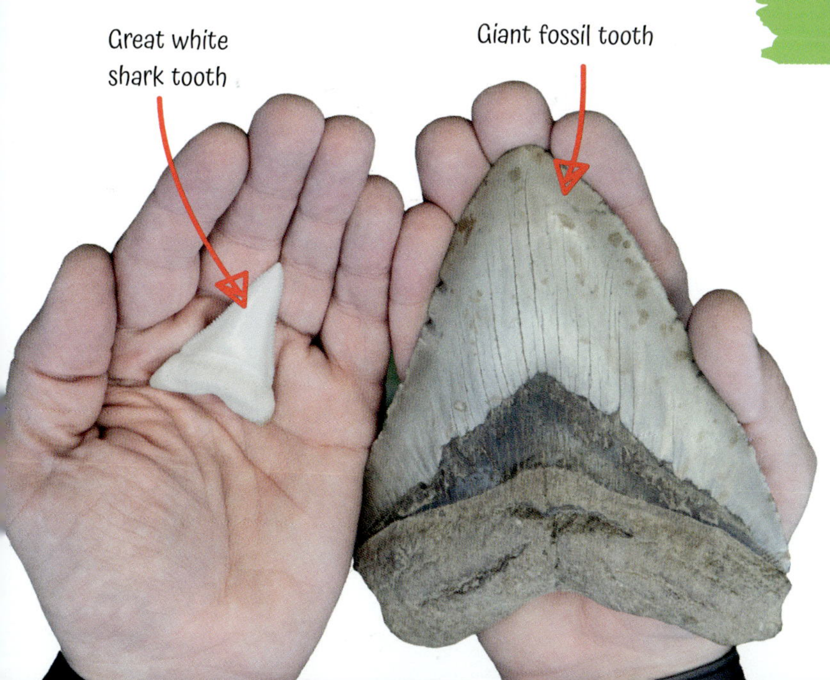

Not much to go on …

Sometimes, one small part of a living thing can be enough to identify a new species. Take this fossil tooth. It's a shark tooth, similar to millions of other fossil shark teeth, and the teeth of sharks living today. But it's much, much bigger.

This means there must have been a very large shark species swimming around between about 23 million and 3 million years ago. It's been nicknamed Megalodon, meaning "Big tooth."

Fighting dinosaurs

Once in a while, a fossil is found showing extinct animals in action, revealing clues about how they behaved. One of these is the "Fighting Dinosaurs," one of the most famous fossil finds in the world.

The Fighting Dinosaurs were found in the Djadochta Formation in the Gobi Desert in southern Mongolia, an important site for dinosaur fossils.

Desert dinosaurs

In the 1960s and 1970s, a team of Mongolian and Polish paleontologists, led by Professor Zofia Kielan-Jaworowska, carried out a series of fossil hunting expeditions in the Gobi Desert. They found dozens of dinosaur fossils, including, in August 1971, the "Fighting Dinosaurs." The fossil skeletons of a *Protoceratops* and a *Velociraptor* were discovered tangled together, in the middle of a battle.

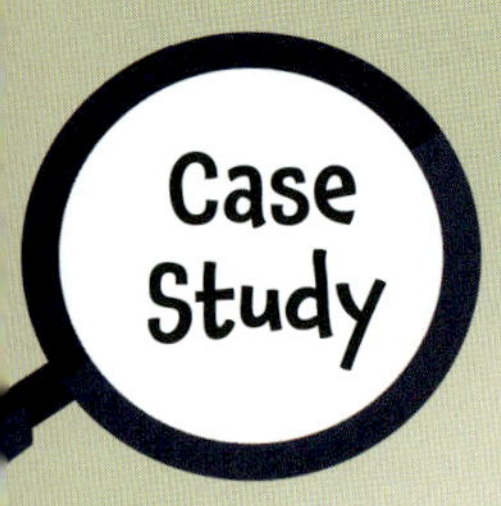

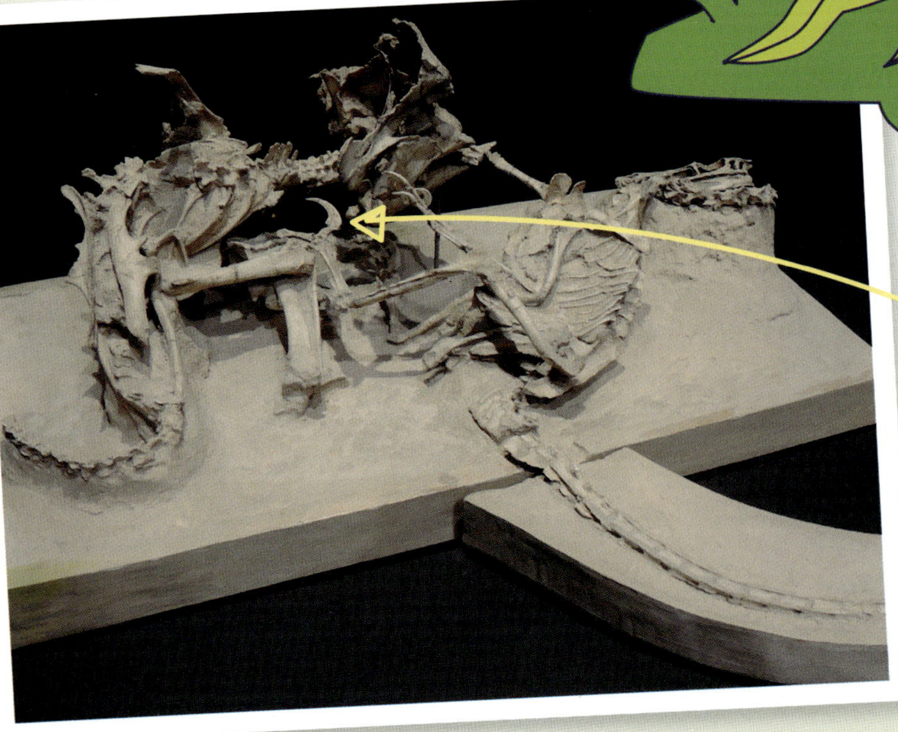

The *Velociraptor's* huge toe claw is jammed into the neck of the *Protoceratops*, which is biting the *Velociraptor's* arm as it struggles on the ground.

Today, the "Fighting Dinosaurs" are on display in the Mongolian Dinosaur Museum in Ulan Bator, Mongolia's capital.

The real-life fight might have looked something like this. *Velociraptor* and *Protoceratops* were both small-to-medium-sized dinosaurs, about 6 feet (1.8 m) long.

Trapped in time

It's very rare for dinosaurs to die and become fossilized in the middle of a fight like this. Paleontologists aren't sure what happened. One theory is that a huge pile of sand suddenly slipped down a nearby sand dune, burying the dinosaurs in an instant. They didn't have time to try to escape, or even move from their mid-fight position.

FACT FILE

THE FIGHTING DINOSAURS

SPECIES: *PROTOCERATOPS ANDREWSI* AND *VELOCIRAPTOR MONGOLIENSIS*

LOCATION: GOBI DESERT, MONGOLIA

DISCOVERED: 1971

AGE: AROUND 80 MILLION YEARS OLD

WHO WOULD HAVE WON?

These dinosaurs were pretty evenly matched in size, so if they hadn't been buried in a sand avalanche, how would the fight have ended? We know *Velociraptor* was a fierce hunter, and often attacked plant-eaters like *Protoceratops*. But *Protoceratops* was armed with big, powerful beak-like jaws for fighting back. As they had both managed to injure each other, a fight like this could have ended up with both dinosaurs dead.

SOLVING PUZZLES

Being a paleontologist can be like being a detective. You have to piece together clues and search for evidence to find out what a prehistoric creature looked like and how it lived.

Iguanodon's nose

In 1822, British paleontologist Gideon Mantell discovered the first known fossils of the dinosaur *Iguanodon* – a few very large teeth. As they looked like the teeth of iguana lizards (but much bigger), Mantell named the species *Iguanodon*, or "iguana-tooth."

More bones were discovered, and Mantell tried to fit them together to make a skeleton. When he found a spike-shaped bone, he put it on *Iguanodon's* nose – because some types of iguanas have nose spikes.

Much later, after Mantell had died, several complete Iguanadon fossils were dug up. They showed that each *Iguanodon* had two spikes, and they were actually its thumbs!

? More mysteries

Even today, paleontologists are still trying to find the answers to all kinds of puzzles ...

• What were those thumb spikes for?

We've known about Iguanodons' thumb spikes for over a century, but paleontologists still aren't sure how they used them. Were they for grabbing plants, stabbing enemies, or maybe cracking open nuts?

• How did pterosaurs get off the ground?

Pterosaurs were winged reptiles that lived at the same time as dinosaurs. Some were huge, with enormous heads and wingspans of up to 36 feet (11 m). So how did they get off the ground to start flying?

Did they have to leap off a cliff or run down a hill to get airborne? Or did they push themselves into the air using their wing bones like a pole vault? Or maybe both? Paleontologists have been debating this for years!

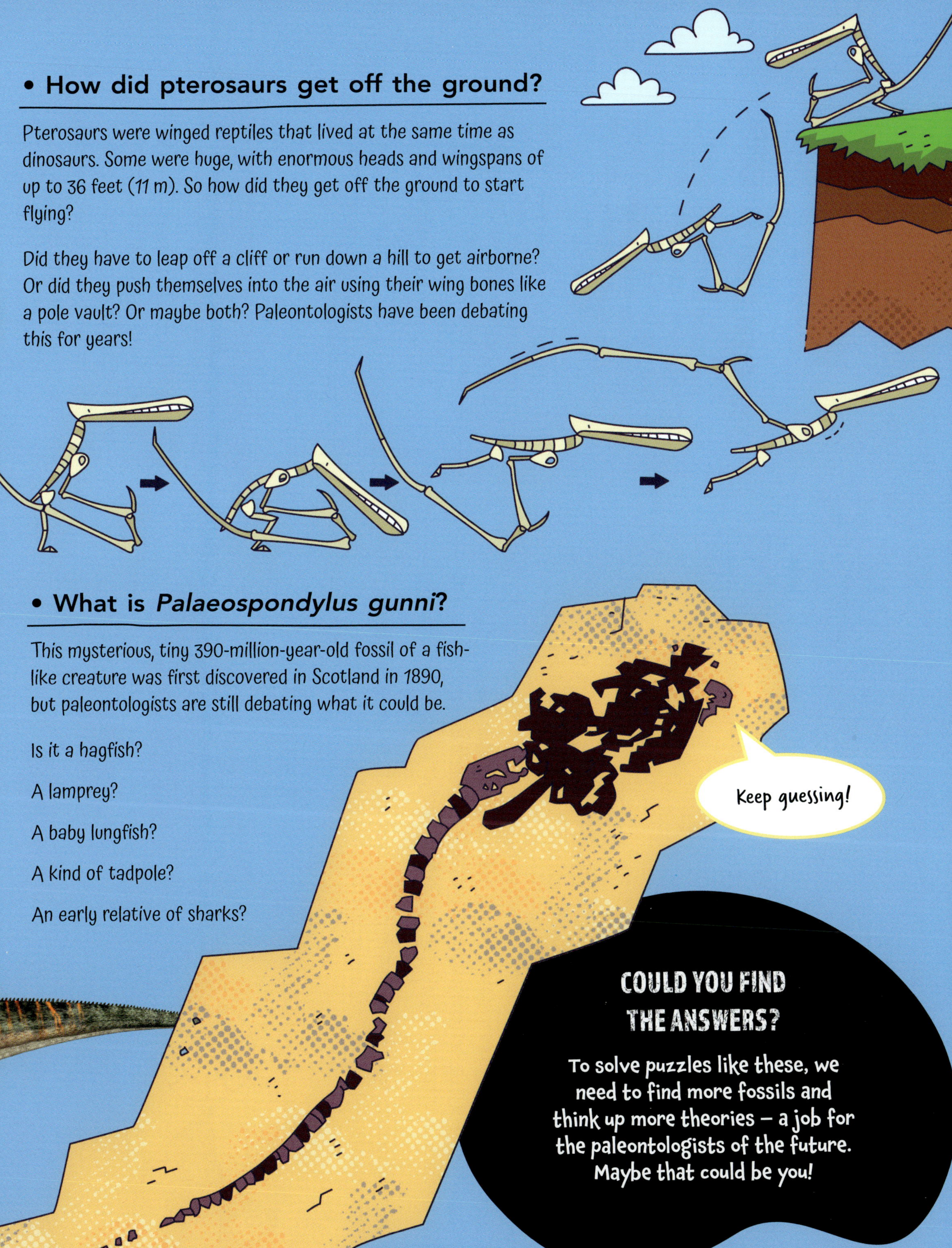

• What is *Palaeospondylus gunni*?

This mysterious, tiny 390-million-year-old fossil of a fish-like creature was first discovered in Scotland in 1890, but paleontologists are still debating what it could be.

Is it a hagfish?

A lamprey?

A baby lungfish?

A kind of tadpole?

An early relative of sharks?

FOSSILS AND EVOLUTION

Evolution is the way living things change over time, and new species appear. Paleontology can trace how this happened in the past, using fossil clues.

How evolution works

Evolution happens because of DNA found inside cells. DNA contains patterns of chemicals that control how each species grows and works, and what it looks like.

As living things grow and reproduce, or have babies, their cells make copies of their DNA to pass on. Sometimes, there's a mistake in a copy, which can change the next generation. If the change is useful – such as better eyesight, for example – it can help the new version of the species to survive. Other random, unimportant DNA changes get passed on too.

In this way, ancient single-celled living things gradually changed and evolved into all the different species that have existed on Earth.

YOUR GREAT-GREAT-GRANDFISH!

Most living things don't become fossils, and fossils can be hard to find – so there are lots of gaps in the fossil record (see page 16). Once in a while, an exciting new fossil find fills in a gap.

In 2010, a 375-million-year-old fish fossil, *Elpistostege*, revealed how five digits evolved inside the fins of early fish. They later evolved into reptile claws, mammal paws, and our own five fingers.

Fossil evidence

The fossil record is also a record of evolution. Dating methods and rock strata show the order fossils formed in, so we can use them to trace how living things have changed and evolved since life on Earth began.

History of the horse

Fossils can also show how particular types of living things evolved. For example, paleontologists have found many early horse fossils from different dates. They show how tiny ancient horses evolved into the modern horse, *Equus*.

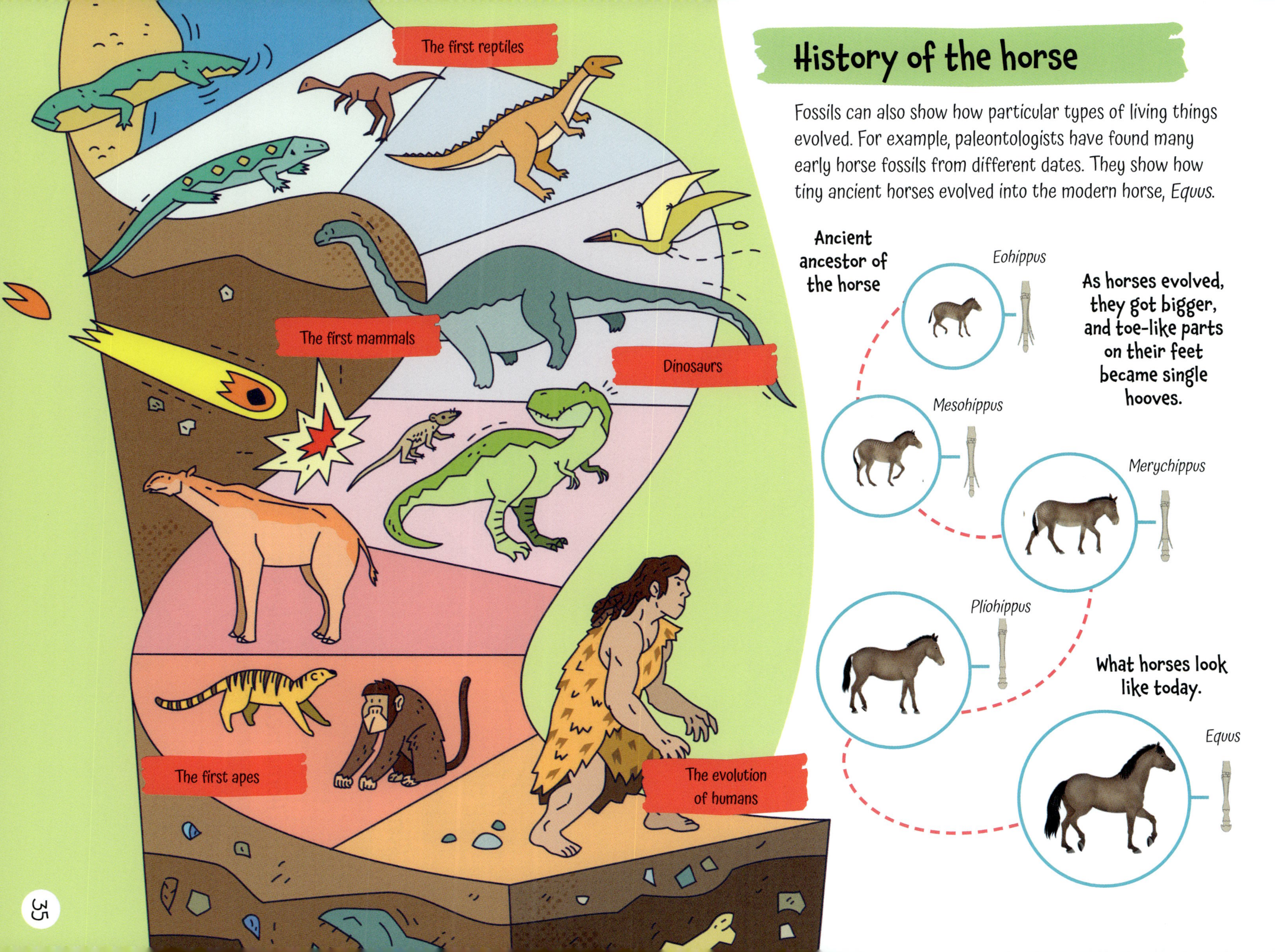

Dragon Man

Fossils can even show us how modern humans like us evolved from earlier types of humans.

The human family

Today there's only one human species, *Homo sapiens*, meaning "smart human." But fossils show that in the past there were several different human species – a whole family tree of humans.

We can't be sure exactly how they were all related, and paleontologists are still finding new human fossils that add to the picture. One of the most recent is *Homo longi*, or "Dragon Man."

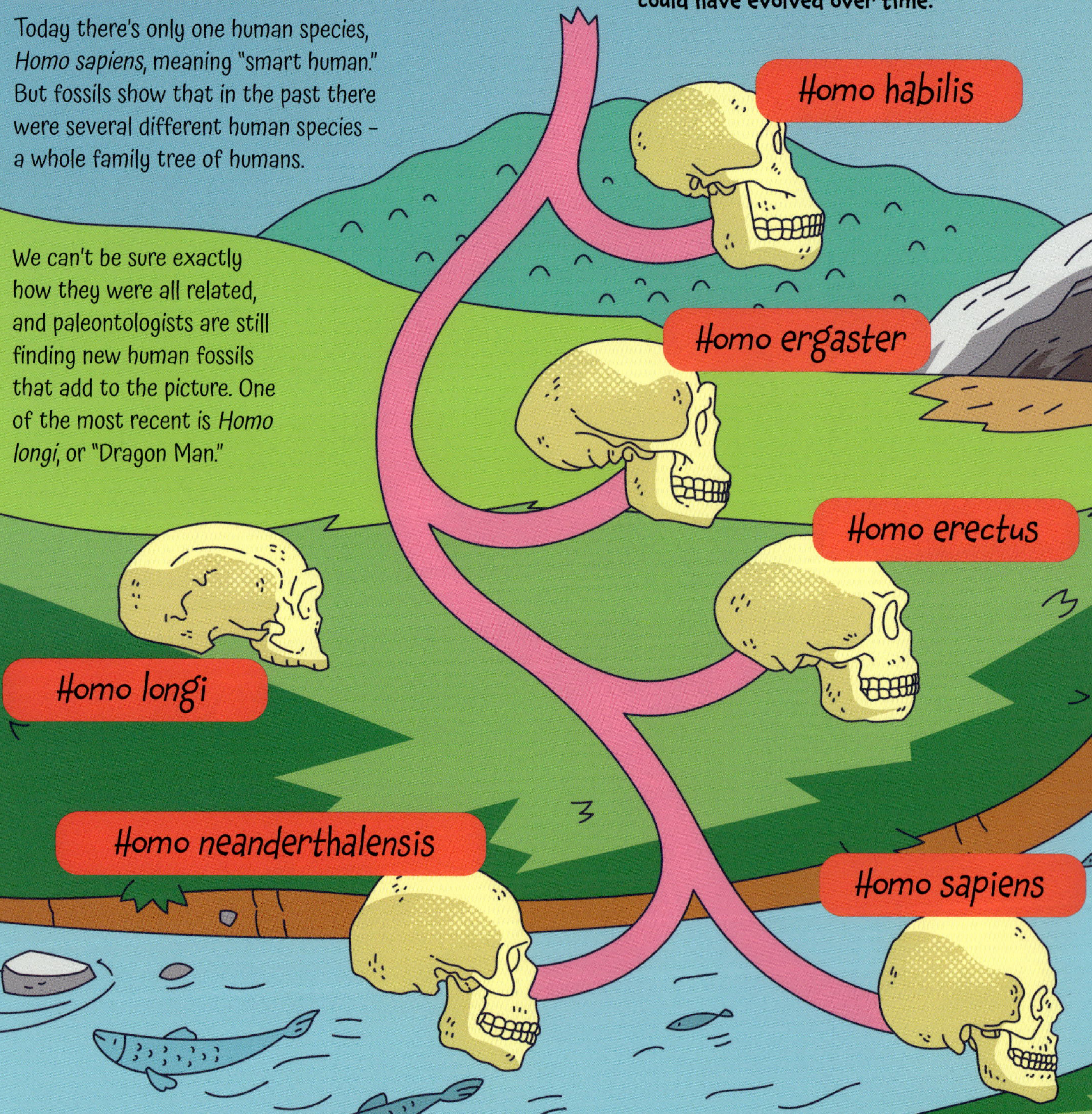

This family tree shows one possible way human species could have evolved over time.

Story of a skull

In 2018, a man handed over a fossil skull to the Hebei University of Geosciences in northwestern China. He claimed his grandfather had found it while building a bridge in the 1930s, and hidden it down a well, only telling his family about it many years later.

When paleontologist Ji Qiang studied the skull, he realized it was a very important discovery. It had space for a large brain, like *Homo sapiens*. But the bone was bigger and thicker, like some earlier human species. Ji decided it was probably a previously unknown species. It was named *Homo longi*, or "Dragon Man," as it was found in the Heilongjiang (Black Dragon River) area of China.

The Dragon Man skull fossil

If *Homo longi* is a separate, newly discovered human species, it was probably closely related either to ourselves, *Homo sapiens*, or to *Homo neanderthalensis* (known as the Neanderthals).

Who was Dragon Man?

Dragon Man was probably around 50 years old, and lived about 146,000 years ago. He may have had a similar life to early *Homo sapiens*, living in a small village and hunting and fishing for food.

FACT FILE

DRAGON MAN

NAME: *HOMO LONGI*

DISCOVERED: 1930s

LOCATION: HEILONGJIANG, CHINA

AGE: 146,000 YEARS OLD

PALEONTOLOGY TECHNOLOGY

Paleontologists today have all kinds of hi-tech tools that weren't available to early pioneers, such as Georges Cuvier, Mary Anning, and Gideon Mantell. Microscopes, scanners, and computers help them discover new fossils and find out more about old ones.

Under the microscope

Microfossils are tiny fossils that are too small to see properly with our eyes alone. Paleontologists use powerful scanning electron microscopes to look for them in rocks, and to make detailed images of them to study.

This scanning electron microscope (SEM) image shows a microfossil mollusk. In real life it's less than 0.08 inch (2 mm) long.

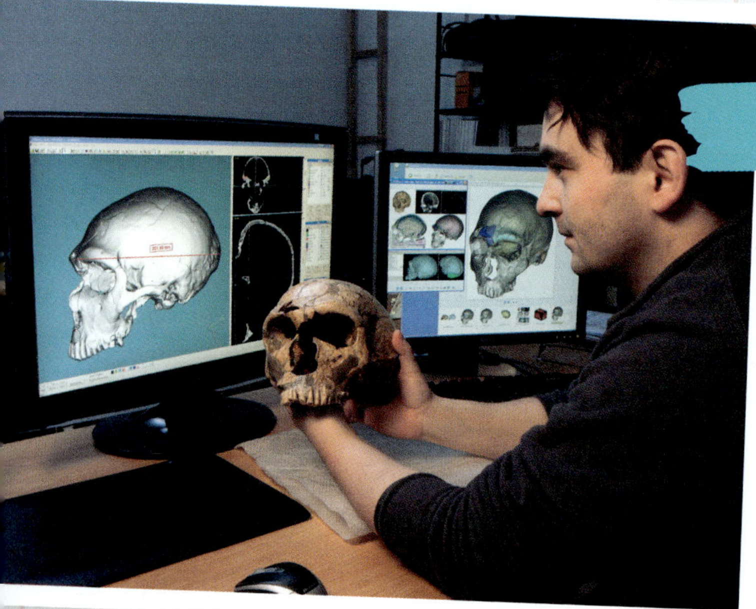

This paleontologist is looking at a scan of a 70,000-year-old fossilized Neanderthal skull.

Looking inside

Some fossils are too delicate to remove from their surrounding rock matrix. Others, like skulls, can have spaces inside that you can't see from the outside. To look inside them, you can use a CT scan, which is a kind of X-ray. It scans the fossil from every angle and builds up a detailed picture of its surfaces and insides, so that paleontologists can look inside it without breaking it apart.

Computer software turns the scan results into a 3D image on a computer screen. You can rotate it, look at it from different angles, use built-in tools to measure it, and look at "slices" cut through it.

Computer simulations

Paleontologists also use scans of fossils to make animated computer simulations of prehistoric animals to model how they might have grown, balanced, or moved – whether that's running, flying, swimming, or slithering.

One simulation created a virtual model of a plesiosaur in a virtual tank of water, to see how it could have used its flippers to swim.

DID YOU KNOW?

Before making the plesiosaur computer simulation, paleontologists tried a real-life experiment – they made model plesiosaur flippers and tied them to human volunteers, who then tried to swim around a swimming pool with them on!

MUSEUMS AND MOVIES

People are fascinated with prehistoric creatures, especially dinosaurs. Some paleontologists use their knowledge to help make museum displays and TV special effects, to explain fossils and ancient life to the public.

Mounting fossils

Mounting a fossil means putting it on display in an exhibition. If it's a big skeleton with lots of parts, this is a huge job for a whole team of workers, including paleontologists, engineers, technicians, and artists. They use strong metal supports and wires to make sure the skeleton is fitted together properly in a realistic position, but is also safe and secure and can't fall on anyone.

Paleontologists and technicians work together to build a dinosaur skeleton display.

Lifelike models

You often see models in museums too, showing you what a prehistoric creature would have looked like in real life. Paleontologists work with artists and modeling companies to make them as realistic as possible.

Meganeura was a griffinfly, related to dragonflies, that lived 300 million years ago. It was one of the biggest insects ever, with a wingspan of up to 28 inches (70 cm). A 3D model can help you imagine what it would be like to meet one!

Special effects

You might have seen movies or TV shows, such as *Jurassic World* or *Walking With Dinosaurs*, with realistic dinosaurs or other prehistoric wildlife roaming around in them. These computer-generated special effects are often based on the computer simulations paleontologists make to study dinosaurs (see page 39). Artists and animators add realistic skin textures, feathers, fur, eyes, and other parts, and animate the models so that the creatures look real.

A Mosasaurus, a huge fierce ocean predator that lived from 145–66 million years ago, features in the movie *Jurassic World*.

On the stage

Computer effects are great on the screen, but what if you want a realistic dinosaur in a stage show? You need a dinosaur suit! These amazingly convincing costumes are built out of lightweight materials so that an actor can wear them and control them from the inside. They look and move like a real dinosaur.

Can you spot the human inside the costume?

COULD PREHISTORIC LIFE REALLY COME BACK?

In movies, such as *Jurassic Park* and *Jurassic World*, scientists create living dinosaurs using ancient DNA recovered from fossils. Could that really happen?

How would it work?

In the movies, the scientists find dinosaur blood inside blood-sucking mosquitoes trapped in amber, and extract DNA from it. They use the DNA to make cloned dinosaurs. To clone an animal, you put its DNA into an egg cell from another animal, and it grows into a baby. This has already been done with sheep and other animals. But would it really work with dinosaurs?

If we did clone dinosaurs, they could be pretty dangerous.

Dino DNA

In real life, it's very hard to collect useful DNA from fossils. There are ancient mosquitoes and other blood-sucking insects trapped in amber. But amber forms under heat and pressure, and this destroys any blood that might be inside a mosquito's stomach.

A different type of mosquito fossil, preserved in mud at the bottom of an ancient lake, has been found with blood still inside it.

But scientists still couldn't find any DNA in the blood cells. That's because DNA is a very delicate substance that breaks down over time. The last dinosaurs died out 66 million years ago, so we're unlikely to find any useful dinosaur DNA.

Making a mammoth

However, scientists have extracted DNA from extinct animals that lived more recently, such as frozen woolly mammoths (see page 15). As mammoths are quite similar to today's elephants, it might eventually be possible to clone a mammoth and implant it into a female elephant, who could then give birth to it.

1 DNA from a frozen mammoth

2 Egg cell from a living elephant

3 Combined and placed in a female elephant's womb.

4 Female elephant gives birth to baby mammoth.

Other scientists are looking at ways to combine mammoth and elephant DNA to make a new species, called a "mammophant."

IS THAT A GOOD IDEA?

Cloning extinct animals raises the question of ethics, or rights and wrongs. Is it OK to bring back an extinct creature? What if it was dangerous to other animals or humans, damaged the habitat we put it in, or was unhappy? What do you think?

IS PALEONTOLOGY YOUR OLOGY?

After reading this book, do you think you might like being a paleontologist? If so, that's great – paleontology needs you! So what can you do to to help yourself get there?

Useful qualities

Anyone can work with fossils, but there are some skills and qualities that can make you especially well-suited to life as a paleontologist. See how many of these apply to you!

• Love rocks and fossils!

You'll spend a LOT of your time looking closely at lumps of rock, so you have to be really into rocks, minerals, and fossils.

• Love the outdoors

Field trips involve trekking, camping, exploring wild places, and getting muddy. It helps to be physically fit too.

• Problem-solver

Paleontology involves a lot of gathering evidence, figuring out what things mean, and coming up with ideas. And if you're wrong, you don't give up – you have to re-think and start again!

• Plenty of patience

You could spend days, weeks, or even years looking for the particular fossils you're interested in. But imagine how exciting it is when you find them!

• Careful and methodical

Paleontologists have to dig carefully, handle fossils carefully, make detailed notes, and be super-organized.

• Team player

You'll often be working in a team, whether in the field, in the lab, or in a museum.

As you get older, you get to choose the school subjects you want to focus on. If you want to be a paleontologist, these subjects are good choices:

Biology, the science of living things.

Math, **computer science**, and other **science subjects** are useful, too.

Then you could study for a degree in **biology**, **botany**, **zoology**, or **geology**, and specialize in **paleontology** for a second degree.

What else could you do?

Besides being a scientific paleontologist at a university, there are lots of other jobs you can do that involve fossils or prehistoric creatures. You could:

- Work in a museum, making fossil displays and explaining paleontology to visitors.

- Be a fossil hunter, finding fossils to sell to scientists, museums, or the public, or run your own fossil shop like Mary Anning.

- Be a fossil curator, looking after a large fossil collection in a museum.

- Work as a fossil preparator, cleaning and preparing fossils.

- Make movies or TV shows about fossils or prehistoric life, working as a producer, expert, or presenter.

- Write informative books, stories, or plays about fossils, dinosaurs, or other ancient creatures.

- Work as an artist, designer, or animator, making prehistoric special effects, robots, or costumes.

- Be an actor starring as a dinosaur in a dino suit!

GLOSSARY

Air scribe A fine-pointed vibrating tool used to clean fossils.

Amber Fossilized tree resin, which can sometimes contain trapped insects or other small animals.

Ammonite A type of extinct sea creature related to octopuses, with a spiral shell.

Amphibian A type of vertebrate animal that lays eggs in water, such as a frog.

Belemnite An extinct squid-like animal with a pointed skeleton, often found as a fossil.

Botany The study of plants.

Canyon A deep, steep-sided valley where a river has cut through rock.

Carbon A type of element, found in coal and in carbon film fossils.

Carbon film fossil A flat, print-like fossil made from the carbon from a living thing.

Cast A copy of a fossil, made by making a mold of the fossil and filling it with plaster.

Cells Tiny units that living things are made of.

Climate The typical or average weather patterns in a particular place, or on Earth as a whole.

Cloning Making an exact living copy of a species using its DNA.

Computer simulation A simulation or copy of a real-life thing or situation, programmed into a computer to help scientists study it.

Coprolite Fossilized poop.

CT (Computerized Tomography) scan A kind of X-ray scan used to look inside fossils.

Deep time The timescale of the whole history of the Earth, its rocks and life-forms.

Dig A site where paleontologists or fossil hunters dig up the ground to look for fossils.

Dinosaur A type of two-legged or four-legged prehistoric reptile. Many dinosaur species grew to huge sizes.

DNA (deoxyribonucleic acid) A chemical found in cells, used to encode instructions that make the cell work.

Ethics The rights and wrongs of a situation, and whether it's OK to do something.

Evolution A process of gradual change over multiple generations of living things.

Excavate To dig something out of the ground, such as a fossil.

Extinct No longer existing, having died out as a species.

Field work Studying or collecting fossils or data in a natural or outdoor place, known as "the field."

Fossil The remains or traces of a prehistoric living thing preserved in rock.

Fossil fuels Fuels such as oil, coal, and gas, which formed from ancient living things.

Fossil record The fossils found so far and the way they are found in different layers of rock, revealing how old each fossil is.

Geological time Another name for deep time.

Geologist A scientist who studies geology.

Geology The study of rocks and minerals and the structure of the Earth.

GPS (Global Positioning System) A way of using satellites and a receiver to locate where in the world you are.

Ichthyosaur A type of prehistoric sea reptile that looked similar to a fish.

Index fossil Any common type of fossil that can show how old the rocks around it are.

Invertebrate An animal without a backbone.

Jacket A coating of fabric and plaster, used to protect fossils while they are being transported.

Jackhammer A hand-held power tool used to break apart hard rocks.

Lab Short for laboratory, a room or building where scientists do tests or experiments.

Latin name A unique two-part scientific name written in Latin, given to each species.

Mammal A type of vertebrate animal that feeds its young on milk from the mother's body.

Matrix The rock surrounding a fossil, which may be difficult to remove.

Microbe A very small living thing that we can only see using a microscope.

Microfossil A very small fossil that has to be studied using a microscope.

Minerals Pure, natural, non-living substances, such as metals, quartz, and salt.

Modeling Making a model of a real-life situation or thing to help you study it.

Mold fossil A fossil that forms when minerals fill up an empty space in rock, left by a dead creature that has rotted or dissolved away.

Paleontologist Someone who studies paleontology.

Paleontology The study of fossils and what they reveal about prehistoric life.

Paper A written report or essay about your scientific work or discoveries.

Permineralization One of the most common ways for fossils to form, when minerals dissolved in water soak into bones, shells, or other hard parts of living things.

Petrify The scientific word for turning something to stone.

Plesiosaur A type of prehistoric sea reptile, usually with four flippers and a long neck and tail.

Prehistoric Dating from the time before people began to write down historic records.

Preparation Unwrapping, cleaning, and mending fossils to get them ready to be studied.

Preparator Someone whose job is preparing fossils.

Pterosaur A type of prehistoric flying reptile, with wings made from stretched skin.

Quarry A place where lots of rock has been mined or dug out of the ground.

Radiometric dating A way to calculate the age of a rock by measuring radioactive elements found in it

Reptile A type of vertebrate animal, such as a snake, that usually has scales, breathes air, and lays eggs.

Sediment Mud, sand, or other material that settles in layers, usually at the bottom of a liquid.

Sedimentary rocks Rocks made of layers of hardened sediment.

Species A particular type of living thing.

Strata Layers of rock formed and laid down over time, with the oldest rocks in the lowest layers.

Trace fossils Fossilized imprints or marks left by living things, such as dinosaur footprints.

Trilobite A type of very common prehistoric sea creature, related to crabs and insects.

Unaltered remains Remains of prehistoric animals that have not rotted away, for example because they have been frozen in ice.

Vertebrate An animal with a backbone.

Zoology The study of animals.

Further reading

BOOKS

Fossil Hunter: How Mary Anning Changed the Science of Prehistoric Life
by Cheryl Blackford (Clarion Books, 2022)

Paleontologist
by Rosie Banks (Scientific American Educational Publishing, 2025)

Prehistory
by Robert Muir-Wood (Cavendish Square Publishing, 2025)

WEBSITES

Paleontology: The Big Dig
Fun fossil info, games, and activities from the American Museum of Natural History.
https://www.amnh.org/explore/ology/paleontology

Fossils, Facts and Finds
Fascinating facts and photos to help you find out about a wide range of fossils.
https://www.fossils-facts-and-finds.com/

Natural History Museum Dino Directory
Facts about hundreds of dinosaur species for dino fans!
https://www.nhm.ac.uk/discover/dino-directory.html

INDEX